NOSTRADAMUS

BY TONY DOFT

Are you ready to take it to the extreme?
Torque books thrust you into the action-packed world
of sports, vehicles, mystery, and adventure. These books
may include dirt, smoke, fire, and dangerous stunts.
WARNING: read at your own risk.

This edition first published in 2011 by Bellwether Media, Inc.

No part of this publication may be reproduced in whole or in part without written permission of the publisher. For information regarding permission, write to Bellwether Media, Inc., Attention: Permissions Department, 5357 Penn Avenue South, Minneapolis, MN 55419.

Library of Congress Cataloging-in-Publication Data

Doft, Tony.
 Nostradamus / by Tony Doft.
   p. cm. -- (Torque: The unexplained)
 Summary: "Engaging images accompany information about Nostradamus. The combination of high-interest subject matter and light text is intended for students in grades 3 through 7"--Provided by publisher.
 Includes bibliographical references and index.
 ISBN 978-1-60014-584-1 (hardcover : alk. paper)
 1. Nostradamus, 1503-1566--Juvenile literature. I. Title.
 BF1815.N8D643 2011
 133.3092--dc22   2010034777

Printed in the United States of America, North Mankato, MN.

010111   1176

CONTENTS

CHAPTER 1
A TERRIBLE VISION

King Henry II

King Henry II of France went to a **jousting** tournament in the summer of 1559. He planned on jousting a young Scottish captain named Gabriel Montgomery. Jousting was a common sport at the time. Men rode toward each other on horses. They used long, wooden **lances** to try to knock each other to the ground. Few people thought King Henry was in any danger.

Nostradamus thought differently. He was an **adviser** to the king's wife, Queen Catherine. Nostradamus told the queen that he had seen a **vision** of the king's death at the jousting tournament. The queen asked King Henry not to compete, but the king ignored the warning.

When Nostradamus saw his vision of King Henry II's death, he wrote:

The young lion will overcome the older one,
On the field of combat in a single battle;
He will pierce his eyes through a golden cage,
Two wounds made one, then he dies a cruel death.

During the joust, Montgomery's lance broke when it hit King Henry's armor. A large piece of the lance shot up toward the king's head. It went through the golden **visor** that protected the king's face. Another piece went into his throat. King Henry suffered for ten days before he died. The people of France were shocked, but Nostradamus was not surprised. His vision had proven true.

CHAPTER 2

WHO WAS NOSTRADAMUS?

N ostradamus was born in France in 1503. He claimed to be a **seer** after he had his first vision in 1547. He said that God showed him visions of future events so that he could warn people about them. Nostradamus wrote what he saw in verses called **quatrains**. He put them in a book called *Les Propheties*, which means "The **Prophecies**." His fame grew as some of his predictions came true. He wrote more than 942 quatrains during his lifetime.

Nostradamus died in 1566. It is said he knew which day he was going to die. The predictions he left behind live on to this day. People continue to read his quatrains. They believe that many of his predictions have yet to come true.

DR. NOSTRADAMUS

Nostradamus studied medicine and became a doctor. He later studied astrology. This is the belief that the positions of the planets and stars affect people's lives.

CHAPTER 3
SEARCHING FOR ANSWERS

Could Nostradamus see into the future? Some people believe that he could. People still claim to be seers today. They believe they have a special sense that most people lack. This sense allows them to see future events.

Skeptics believe that Nostradamus did not see the future. They doubt any human has that ability. Some skeptics point out that the quatrains Nostradamus wrote are not specific. They say the quatrains can be linked to many events because of their **vague** language. Skeptics also argue that Nostradamus wrote so many predictions that a few were bound to come true.

Believers point to quatrains with dates to prove predictions. In 1666, the Great Fire of London destroyed more than half of the city. Many argue this quatrain predicted the fire:

The blood of the just will be demanded of London,
Burnt by the fire in the year '66
The ancient Lady will fall from her high place
And many of the same sect will be killed.

FAMOUS PREDICTIONS

Many people believe these 10 events were predicted by some of Nostradamus' most famous quatrains.

Year	
1559	
1566	
1666	
1776	
1789	
1929	
1930s	
1940s	
1969	
1986	

Event

The death of King Henry II of France
in a jousting tournament

Nostradamus' own death

The Great Fire of London

The American Revolution

The French Revolution

The United States stock market crash
that led to the Great Depression

The rise of German dictator Adolf Hitler
and the beginning of World War II

The invention and use of the atomic bomb

The *Apollo 11* moon landing

The explosion of the space shuttle *Challenger*

Nostradamus wrote his quatrains by hand and in French. Many skeptics say that people translating the quatrains into English make small changes to make them appear more accurate.

The debate over Nostradamus' predictions will continue. If Nostradamus could see into the future, could any of his quatrains help us prepare for future events? Many of his quatrains are dark and violent. They predict fires, earthquakes, wars, and deaths. Could we use his writings to avoid these disasters, or is there no way to escape the future?

GLOSSARY

adviser—someone who offers advice and helps people make decisions

jousting—a contest in which two people use lances to try to knock each other off horses

lances—long, pointed weapons

prophecies—predictions about what will happen in the future

quatrains—verses written in four lines

seer—a person who claims to see future events

skeptics—people who do not believe in something

vague—not specific; some people argue that many of Nostradamus' quatrains are vague and can apply to many events.

vision—a dreamlike picture seen in the mind; seers often claim to have visions of the future.

visor—a part of a helmet that fits over and protects the face

TO LEARN MORE

AT THE LIBRARY

Doeden, Matt. *Nostradamus*. Mankato, Minn.: Capstone Press, 2007.

Roberts, Russell. *The Life and Times of Nostradamus*. Hockessin, Del.: Mitchell Lane Publishers, 2008.

Stone, Adam. *ESP*. Minneapolis, Minn.: Bellwether Media, 2011.

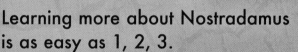

ON THE WEB

Learning more about Nostradamus is as easy as 1, 2, 3.

1. Go to www.factsurfer.com.

2. Enter "Nostradamus" into the search box.

3. Click the "Surf" button and you will see a list of related Web sites.

With factsurfer.com, finding more information is just a click away.

INDEX